# PREMARITAL
# QUESTIONNAIRE
# WORKBOOK

*Premarital Questionnaire Workbook*

Copyright © 2019 Charles Quinn . All Rights Reserved.

ISBN:   978-1-63308-478-0 (paperback)
        978-1-63308-479-7 (ebook)

Cover and Interior Design by *R'tor John D. Maghuyop*

1028 S Bishop Avenue, Dept. 178
Rolla, MO 65401

Printed in United States of America

# PREMARITAL QUESTIONNAIRE WORKBOOK

## CHARLES QUINN

ZOE LIFE LLC

CHALFANT ECKERT
PUBLISHING

# TABLE OF CONTENTS

# PREMARITAL COUNSELING

# PROLOGUE

This questionnaire is designed to present daily interaction questions and concerns that the majority of relationships encounter. Although not exhaustive, it covers a significant portion of issues that couples face. It is intended to highlight any nurturing differences or similarities, and to establish and strengthen compatibility. When brought out and discussed aforetime, there are no assumptions of meaning, and you are better prepared to forge ahead with clarity of mind because you understand your partner's ideology, cultural mindset, and intent on specific issues. This questionnaire will bring awareness and better prepare you for any differences in meaning of words, expectations, and unspoken desires, as well as ensure that your partnership highlights concerns, requests, likes, and dislikes.

These questions are questions many couples fail to ask one another before consummating a partnership. These questions are important because many times unspoken expectations and assumptions bring frustration and eruptions in the partnership. Once again, although not exhaustive, these questions are designed for open discussion and to familiarize you with the language and intrinsic cultures of one another. We don't always convey the message we think we do when communicating with each other. We come from many different environments, households, cultures, and backgrounds. So, my prayer is as you discuss these questions in open dialog, take into consideration the differences, and this will prepare you both for a happy and exciting journey of a lifetime in Holy Matrimony.

The institution of marriage is very sacred; it is a covenant agreement between two people on display, demonstrating a greater storyline: one of patience, one of perpetual forgiveness, one of not just being loved, but one of learning how to give love, one that shows forth God's love for the church.

I have seen great marriages prosper and I have seen some great marriages fail, and you might wonder how if it failed, it could be called great. Because two great people can come together, with great ideas of a long life together, but due to non-defining defaults and lack of clarity, these potentially great unions failed. One quick example: If two people come together with a single idea of having a great marriage but fail to define each one's ideas of a great marriage, that potentially great marriage starts off with great intents, but lacks an accurate understanding of what each defining statement of a 'happy marriage' means. If no query is made, although the same words are used, different meanings are lived out. Even the word *love* has a different meaning to each individual. So, before you enter into this sacred covenant, invest a few minutes into this probing questionnaire to determine if your partner understands your cultural meanings as you articulate your heart.

# PREMARITAL COUNSELING

# INSTRUCTIONS

This questionnaire is designed for those who desire to know one another more intentionally, intrinsically, and more intimately or even for those who are already married. Even if you decide not to involve a professional or experienced marriage counselor, **please complete the form individually** and then come together after completing the entire form to discuss your answers openly and honestly (preferably with an experienced marriage counselor). The more openness and honesty now, the fewer ill-revelations later.

You both are unique individuals, so differences in meanings of words and phrases are inevitable. When simple, unintentional misunderstanding of meaning occurs, with most couples, this brings about conflict, frustration, or negative perceptions that grow over time. It is my prayer and hope that this questionnaire (if answered honestly and without fear of hurting or offending) will alleviate or lessen the destructive conflict and produce a productive partnership. Marriage is work, and it takes understanding, comparison, compromise, the benefit of the doubt, love, patience, and most of all God, to bring two unique individuals together with common goals to grow into one true union. So, let's get started.

These questions are an investment into not just one happy day of your life, but the beginning of many happy days. It is well worth you taking your time and completing each question with an honest heart. Men, the ladies don't need a one-time savior, that role is taken. They need a lifelong partner. So, take your time and complete the entire questionnaire and come together afterward and be open and honest with each other. You will be glad you did.

Lastly, answer each question to the best of your ability, even if you do not fully understand the question. Your point of view of each subject will point out intuitive differences that will generate deeper insight.

# PREMARITAL COUNSELING
## ZOE LIFE LLC

Name: _____

Phone #: _____

Email: _____

DOB: _____

Employer: _____

Educational level: _____

Notes:

_____

_____

_____

_____

_____

_____

_____

_____

# GAINING INSIGHT

1.  What is your definition of *love*?

    _____

    _____

    _____


2.  Why marriage? In other words, why do you feel that marriage is right for you
    at this time and this is the right person for you?

    _____

    _____

    _____

    _____


3.  What do you think are some requirements for a stable marriage?

    _____

    _____

    _____


4.  In your opinion, what is the super-glue for any marriage that keeps it together
    forever?

    _____

    _____

    _____

    _____

5. What are your definitions of respect and submission?

_____

_____

_____

_____

6. What is meant by *mutual submission*?

_____

_____

_____

_____

7. What are some of your expectations from your spouse and from this union?

_____

_____

_____

8. What do you feel you have to offer to your future spouse?

_____

_____

_____

9. Who wants kids? How many?

_____

_____

_____

10. *My responsibilities, my role, and my lane:* In your opinion, do males have different roles in marriage than females? What are those roles? Explain your preferences.

_____

_____

_____

11. Do you like doing things together or mostly apart?

_____

_____

_____

12. What do you like to do most with your time off?

_____

_____

_____

13. What is your favorite way to spend an evening?

_____

_____

_____

14. Name three things you and your spouse-to-be have in common.

_____

_____

_____

15. What are three positive characteristics of your partner?

_____

_____

_____

16. If you had to change something about your partner, what would it be?

_____

_____

_____

17. *In every relationship there should be relating.* What does that statement mean to you?

_____

_____

_____

18. What does *to death do us part* mean to you?

_____

_____

_____

19. If you have an issue on your heart, do you prefer sharing it or analyzing it intrinsically?

_____

_____

_____

20. What are your partner's likes and dislikes?

_____

_____

_____

21. *Correct me in love with respect to build me up and not tear me down.* What does that statement mean to you?

_____

_____

_____

22. In your opinion, what does it take to make a marriage work (*thrive* not just survive)?

_____

_____

_____

23. What is the role of the Head of the Household, or should there be a head?

_____

_____

_____

24. What is your idea of a happy marriage?

_____

_____

_____

25. What does the word *Trust* mean to you and how important is it to a marriage?

_____

_____

_____

26. What does the word *Commitment* mean to you and how important is it to a marriage?

_____

_____

_____

# FEELING LOVED

1.  Out of the six areas listed below, which one or two do you feel you respond to most positively? (I Corinthians 4-8)

    ____ When someone is saying positive expressions to you about you
    ____ When someone is spending time with you, focusing on the two of you
    ____ Receiving things
    ____ Your partner doing things that need to be done around the home
    ____ The touch of closeness by someone close to you
    ____ Deep personal talks

2.  How important is it to you to spend time together? How much time is enough? Is there a perfect time? When is a bad time? Is it possible to spend too much time together? Explain.

    _____
    _____
    _____
    _____
    _____
    _____
    _____
    _____
    _____
    _____

3. Feelings I have difficulty expressing to my partner include (i.e. fear, inadequacy, jealousy, crying, give her/him compliments, anger, failure, praising God out loud, tenderness, romance, etc.):

_____

_____

_____

_____

4. I really like it when my fiancé shows his/her love for me by (complete this statement):

_____

_____

_____

_____

5. I would really like it if my fiancé would also (complete this statement):

_____

_____

_____

_____

6. I would like for us to do these things together:

\_\_\_\_ Participate in sports together

\_\_\_\_ Watch sports together

\_\_\_\_ Have romantic evenings together

____ Play games at home

____ Share jokes or humor

____ Go to plays, concerts, movies

____ I like/I don't want surprises/being surprised

____ Working together to fix things up

____ Share household cleaning

____ Workout together

____ Have our own friends

____ Still go on dates

____ Save money for vacations

____ Go to counseling often

____ Eat out often

____ Walks in the park often

7. Complete the following sentence: I feel loved when

_____

_____

_____

_____

8. List three things your fiancé has done or can do that helps/would help you feel loved and appreciated.

_____

_____

_____

_____

9.  What do you expect of a marital partner in terms of emotional support during times of insecurity, excitement, depression, illness, and loss?

_____

_____

_____

_____

10. What do you feel your partner needs to do to maintain your love and trust?

_____

_____

_____

11. Do you think it's important to communicate during the day? Explain.

_____

_____

_____

_____

12. If one of us is late or plans change, do you think it's important to communicate with each other? (This is not a *trust issue, but an issue of caring for the other person.) *If you have trust issues due to past relationships, please express that openly and upfront.

_____

_____

_____

_____

# PREVIOUS RELATIONSHIPS AND MARRIAGES

1. Is this your first marriage? Yes or No

2. If No, briefly describe how your last marriage ended and what role you feel you played in the dissolving of that union?

   _____

   _____

   _____

   _____

3. Is there still interaction between you and your ex-husband/ex-wife? Describe the interaction and frequency.

   _____

   _____

   _____

   _____

4. If there are kids from a previous relationship, what role, if any, do you expect your spouse-to-be to play in their lives?

   _____

   _____

   _____

   _____

5. Sometimes when you enter a new relationship, you bring baggage from previous relationships. Many individuals enter relationships and begin to reprimand their new partner for things their past partner(s) did. What are your thoughts on that?

_____

_____

_____

_____

6. Do you carry any ill feelings from previous relationships? Explain.

_____

_____

_____

_____

7. *Do you feel that you are healed from all past relationships?* Explain.

_____

_____

_____

_____

8. Do you feel you are healed from your past traumas and hurts?

_____

_____

_____

(We can get help together).

# FAMILY HISTORY AND INFLUENCE

1. Are your parents still married? Yes or No

2. Did/do your parents get along? Describe their relationship and what you think about it.

   _____

   _____

   _____

   _____

3. Was verbal or physical abuse part of your parents' relationship? If yes, explain.

   _____

   _____

   _____

   _____

4. Do you or any of your family members have or have had psychiatric, emotional, or substance use issues/disorders? If yes, describe the disorder and who had it.

   _____

   _____

   _____

   _____

5. How close and affectionate are you and your family?

_____

_____

_____

6. How do you feel about your relationship with your mother (answered by male)/your father (to be answered by female)?

_____

_____

_____

7. How was your childhood?

_____

_____

_____

8. Briefly describe how you were raised.

_____

_____

_____

9. What type of relationship do you have with your fiancé's family? Do you feel accepted? Do you accept them? Describe the relationship.

_____

_____

_____

10. What role, if any, should your parental families play in your new lives together (involvement/outside influences)?

_____

_____

_____

_____

11. *Two becoming one*: Please read Genesis 2:24 from the Bible and write down your opinion of what that verse means.

_____

_____

_____

_____

# PRECONCEPTIONS AND MISCONCEPTIONS

1.  What role does a husband play in the marriage? (Priest of the home Ephesians 5:23), head of the household, or equal roles?

    _____

    _____

    _____

    _____

    _____

2.  What role does a wife play in the marriage? (Please read the following Scriptures: 1 Corinthians 7:2; 1 Peter 3:1; Ephesians 5:25). Please give your opinion.

    _____

    _____

    _____

    _____

3.  Giving 100%, instead of 50/50: In the marriage, please state your opinion and explain your preference.

    _____

    _____

    _____

    _____

4.  (Female) Mutual decision-making still requires someone to make a final decision. Do you trust this person to make decisions for you and your household? If no, explain.

_____

_____

_____

_____

5.  Will divorce be an option if irreconcilable issues arise? Explain.

_____

_____

_____

6.  How do you feel about negative-character jokes about you in public?

_____

_____

_____

_____

7.  How important is it to you that your spouse stay persuadable (stay interesting, stay exciting, keep themselves up, stay mentally and physically attractive, stay friends)?

_____

_____

_____

_____

8. How do you feel about strong-willed women? How do you feel about passive males?

_____

_____

_____

_____

9. Tradition has it that males are the custodians of outside chores, and women are the custodians of chores inside the house. What are your thoughts?

_____

_____

_____

10. What holidays do you celebrate, how do you celebrate them, and are there any you don't celebrate? Are your ideas of holiday celebrations compatible with your partner's ideas? Explain.

_____

_____

_____

11. How important it is to you that we watch what we say in front of the kids? I want you and I to be their hero.

_____

_____

_____

_____

# POTENTIAL ISSUES

1. Do you currently have any of these concerns or issues?

____ Academic school problems

____ Bankruptcy

____ Relational problems
other than family

____ Divorce

____ Financial difficulty

____ Legal issues

____ Sexual issues

____ Any Medical issues

____ Mama/Daddy drama

____ Alcoholism - self/family member

____ Parenting style differences

____ Workplace problems

____ Disability

____ Any trauma experiences

____ Spiritual issues

____ Miscarriage

____ Drug issues

____ Any Diseases

2. Do you have a history of substance use? If yes, explain.

_____

_____

_____

_____

3. Have you ever sought treatment for substance use? If yes, explain.

_____

_____

_____

_____

4. Have you ever received any counseling or other mental health services? If yes, when did that occur and what was the reason?

_____

_____

_____

_____

5. What are some things that your spouse-to-be is doing now that you feel could become issues later on in the relationship?

_____

_____

_____

_____

6. What past or closet issues your spouse-to-be does not know about might arise later in the marriage and cause a problem?

_____

_____

_____

_____

_____

7. What are your religious views and is it important to you that the family participate in your views?

_____

_____

_____

_____

_____

8. Are you a person who likes to talk about your emotions or keep them to yourself? (introvert/extrovert)

_____

_____

_____

_____

_____

9. What are some things about yourself that you don't like? (Some suggested areas are listed below)

| | | | |
|---|---|---|---|
| ____ | Controlling | ____ | Introvert |
| ____ | Clingy | ____ | Take things to heart |
| ____ | Low Self-Esteem | ____ | Analytical |
| ____ | Rejection | ____ | Procrastinator |
| ____ | Perfectionist | ____ | Jealous |
| ____ | Judgmental | ____ | Lazy |
| ____ | Very Opinionated | ____ | Insecure |
| ____ | Materialistic | ____ | Non-trusting |
| ____ | Extrovert | ____ | Quick Temper |

Others: _____

# DISAGREEMENTS

1. How do you deal with conflicts?

   _____

   _____

   _____

2. During arguments (passionate discussions), do you confront for immediate resolutions or do you prefer retreating to think about it before responding?

   _____

   _____

   _____

   _____

3. How do you resolve disagreements?

   _____

   _____

   _____

   _____

4. What do you fear most and how does that fear influence your anger?

   _____

   _____

   _____

   _____

5.  Complete this statement: When I feel really angry with my partner, I usually...

———————————————————————————————————

———————————————————————————————————

———————————————————————————————————

———————————————————————————————————

———————————————————————————————————

———————————————————————————————————

6.  What do you do when you are having a disagreement?

____    Argue

____    Hit Things

____    Fight

____    Retreat to be alone

____    Get Very Angry

____    Use Profanity

____    Confront

____    Get Loud

____     Retreat to a Drink

____    Take a Drive

____    Pull Away

____    Leave the Area or Leave Home

____    Plot Revenge

____    Talk to my Bio-family

____    Talk to my friends

Other reactions to disagreements: _____

7. If you can't seem to resolve a problem with your spouse, what course of action would you take?

_____

_____

_____

8. What are some behaviors that your fiancé has that you do not like?

_____

_____

_____

_____

9. Although things might sound one way, seek clarity before you form an opinion and make a negative statement. What does this statement mean to you?

_____

_____

_____

_____

10. You can win the argument, but lose the heart in the process. What does that statement mean to you? (We make decisions not to be just right, but to be effective for the whole).

_____

_____

_____

_____

11. The foundations for many arguments are misunderstandings. What do you feel are some good ways to clear up misunderstandings?

_____

_____

_____

_____

12. Yes or No: It is easy for you to express your emotions.

_____

_____

_____

_____

13. Judge my heart, not my actions: In your opinion what does this statement mean?

_____

_____

_____

_____

14. Neither of you are perfect, expect some flaws. What does this statement mean to you?

_____

_____

_____

_____

15. Don't always be so predictable, keep the mystery alive. What does this statement mean to you?

_____

_____

_____

_____

16. Anyone can yell, but honey is sweeter and more attractive. What does that statement mean to you?

_____

_____

_____

_____

17. Create new possibilities when conflicts arise. Work together to brainstorm new options. What do these statements mean to you?

_____

_____

_____

_____

18. Do you apologize when you are wrong?

_____

_____

_____

_____

19. Can I be open and honest with you without you acting upon your feelings?

_____

_____

_____

20. My words can mean different things to you. Please ask for clarification before getting angry. (Your thoughts)

_____

_____

_____

21. When I make a mistake, no matter how many times, please - I need your support, and not your judgment and criticism. Please guide me with your love and respect.

_____

_____

_____

22. Please, do not teach me that I cannot be open and honest with you. You teach me to bottle up my thoughts and feelings by getting angry, retaliating, judging me, and justifying your actions and words when I tell you my perceived truth, especially if you asked me to be truthful. (Your thoughts)

_____

_____

_____

_____

23. In order for our friendship and love to mature, there must be 'Depth Clarity' and absolute honesty of self-revelation. Depth Clarity and self-revelation involve sharing how you are feeling without any blaming or ill will toward the other person. You are not accusing the other person of being the cause of that particular feeling. You are just sharing how you are feeling at the moment. You are sharing what feeling arose intrinsically because of your partner's actions or words without saying it is their fault you feel that way. (Your thoughts):

_____

_____

_____

_____

_____

_____

# FINANCES

1.  Who will have primary responsibility for bill paying and distribution of funds in the household? (Or will you split the responsibility?)

    _____

    _____

    _____

2.  Will you have separate accounts, a joint account, or both? Explain your preference.

    _____

    _____

    _____

3.  Will you have a family budget plan?

    _____

    _____

    _____

4.  Should each of you have some money, either on a regular basis or on occasion, that is not accountable or that can be spent as desired without the approval of the other spouse?

    _____

    _____

    _____

5. Are you predominantly a spender or a saver? Is your spouse-to-be predominantly a spender or a saver? How do you think this will work out for the two of you? Do you anticipate any issues? If so, what do you anticipate?

_____

_____

_____

_____

_____

6. Do you have any indebtedness? List the debts, amounts, monthly obligation, and current status of payments (current, behind, almost paid off, etc.). Do you expect your spouse-to-be to pay off these debts for you?

_____

_____

_____

_____

_____

7. How were your parents with money? Describe. (Also take in consideration that where they are now may have been a little different when they started out.)

_____

_____

_____

_____

_____

8. Did your parents have any financial issues? Explain.

_____

_____

_____

9. Did both of your parents work?

_____

_____

_____

10. How do you feel about a stay-home spouse?

_____

_____

_____

_____

11. How do you feel about Credit Cards?

_____

_____

_____

12. (Christians) Household Tithes/Offering to your local church. What are your thoughts?

_____

_____

_____

13. Are you a shopper? If so, is it important to get items now or save up for them?

_____

_____

_____

_____

14. Do you like to go on vacations? Describe a good vacation. What dream destinations you would love to visit? How will you save for them?

_____

_____

_____

_____

15. Do you both expect to support the family financially and, if kids are in the future, will that change when kids arrive? Explain.

_____

_____

_____

_____

16. Do you agree to have full financial disclosure about each of your own personal financial situations? Explain.

_____

_____

_____

_____

17. If there are strong disagreements about spending money, how will you resolve them?

_____

_____

_____

_____

18. Are there any debts that either partner has incurred before the marriage (e.g. - college or graduate school loans or credit card debt)? If so, how will you handle them?

_____

_____

_____

_____

19. If you were deeply in debt and needed to make a major improvement in your family finances, how would you do it? Would you be a willing partner in the change? What changes would you be willing to make to eliminate the problem? Would you expect your partner to be totally responsible for handling the financial problems?

_____

_____

_____

_____

_____

_____

20. What are your thoughts on borrowing money from family members? On paying them back?

_____

_____

_____

_____

21. Would bankruptcy ever become an option? Explain.

_____

_____

_____

_____

22. How important is life insurance to you and how much life insurance should each of you have?

_____

_____

_____

_____

23. How important is retirement to you and how much do you think should be put away for retirement?

_____

_____

_____

_____

24. How important is savings to you and how much savings do you think you should have? What could savings be used for?

_____

_____

_____

_____

_____

25. How do you feel about your spouse supporting his/her parent(s) financially?

_____

_____

_____

_____

_____

26. How do you feel about life insurance?

_____

_____

_____

_____

27. How do you feel about saving up for kids' college educations?

_____

_____

_____

_____

# ROMANCE, INTIMACY, AND SEX

1. What is/was your favorite fairy tale? Why is/was it your favorite?

   _____

   _____

   _____

2. What fairy tale most resembles your life? Why do you think so?

   _____

   _____

   _____

3. What is your definition of _romance_ and how often should it occur?

   _____

   _____

   _____

   _____

4. How important is romance to you and what is your expectation/definition of romance? Explain.

   _____

   _____

   _____

   _____

5. What are your thoughts about roses/flower?

_____

_____

_____

_____

6. Should romance be expected/automatic or inflamed by desirability/ *attractiveness/sex appeal? (Your thoughts) *attractiveness is incited by your partner's own desires or deterred by unattractive acts, words, appeal, or the lack of acts of service.

_____

_____

_____

_____

7. What is your definition of *intimacy* and how important is intimacy to you? Explain.

_____

_____

_____

_____

8. Does intimacy always lead to sex? Explain.

_____

_____

_____

9.  How important is sex to you? Explain.

_____

_____

_____

10. What's more important to you: The "lead-up" to intimacy or the intimacy/
    sex? Explain.

_____

_____

_____

_____

11. How often should a couple have sex?

_____

_____

_____

12. What type of boundaries do you have when it comes to sex?

_____

_____

_____

13. Do you have a healthy self-concept about your body? Explain.

_____

_____

_____

14. If your spouse-to-be was ever permanently unable to have sex, what would you do?

_____

_____

_____

_____

15. Have you ever been unfaithful to a partner in the past? What were the circumstances? What was the outcome? What did you learn?

_____

_____

_____

_____

_____

16. If your spouse-to-be was ever unfaithful to you, what would you do?

_____

_____

_____

_____

17. How important is it for your spouse to keep in shape?

_____

_____

_____

_____

18. Is it important to you for your spouse to look good as often as possible? Explain.

_____

_____

_____

_____

19. How does your partner stay attractive to you?

_____

_____

_____

_____

20. What physical qualities are you most attracted to in the opposite sex?

_____

_____

_____

_____

# GOALS AND ASPIRATIONS

1. What have you dreamed about doing with your life? What are the reasons you haven't done it?

   _____

   _____

   _____

   _____

   _____

2. What is most important to you? (You can name several things.)

   _____

   _____

   _____

   _____

   _____

3. What dreams, goals, aspirations, and boundaries are important to you? How important is it that your spouse always respect them?

   _____

   _____

   _____

   _____

   _____

   _____

4. When you look back at the end of your life, what things will you regret or make you feel cheated if you do not achieve or do them?

_____

_____

_____

_____

_____

5. **Do you believe that it is too late or that you are incapable of fulfilling your life-long goals?**

_____

_____

_____

_____

6. **Do you still have dreams and believe in yourself?**

_____

_____

_____

_____

7. **Are you blaming anyone for your unfulfilled dreams and expectations?**

_____

_____

_____

_____

# FRIENDS

1. Do you like to be around friends often, occasionally, seldom, or not at all? Why?

   _____

   _____

   _____

2. If your friends are toxic to the marriage, should you still hang around them? Explain.

   _____

   _____

   _____

3. When you get married, should you still hang with single friends, and if so, how often?

   _____

   _____

   _____

4. What do you value most in a friendship, and what does friendship mean to you?

   _____

   _____

   _____

5. Having a same-gender friend in your life can be very beneficial. Although your spouse-to-be can be your best friend, sometimes you may need to have a man-to-man or woman-to-woman talk. Is it important to you to maintain these types of friendships?

_____

_____

_____

_____

6. *Although men can be very talkative and seemingly good listeners in the beginning, that is not the disposition of most men.* What is your viewpoint on this statement?

_____

_____

_____

7. Is it important to you to have an older mentor couple in your life?

_____

_____

_____

8. How would you feel or how do you feel about your fiancé having friends of the opposite sex? Explain.

_____

_____

_____

9. How do you feel about maintaining friendships with your friends of the opposite sex?

_____

_____

_____

_____

10. How does your spouse-to-be feel about you maintaining friends of the opposite sex?

_____

_____

_____

_____

# VIEWPOINTS SCALE

The object of this short area of interest questionnaire is to get a glimpse of how comparable (near or far) your individual views are about certain areas.

**Please mark one block per question: 1=Totally agree 7=Totally disagree**

| | 1 | 2 | 3 | 4 | 5 | 6 | 7 |
|---|---|---|---|---|---|---|---|
| Religious Interaction is very Important in my life. | ☐ | ☐ | ☐ | ☐ | ☐ | ☐ | ☐ |
| Sharing my feelings is important. | ☐ | ☐ | ☐ | ☐ | ☐ | ☐ | ☐ |
| Outside activities together are Important. | ☐ | ☐ | ☐ | ☐ | ☐ | ☐ | ☐ |
| Showing affection/touching is important. | ☐ | ☐ | ☐ | ☐ | ☐ | ☐ | ☐ |
| During an argument: I shut down. | ☐ | ☐ | ☐ | ☐ | ☐ | ☐ | ☐ |
| During an argument: I say insensitive things. | ☐ | ☐ | ☐ | ☐ | ☐ | ☐ | ☐ |
| During an argument: I leave the house. | ☐ | ☐ | ☐ | ☐ | ☐ | ☐ | ☐ |
| During an argument: I get physical. | ☐ | ☐ | ☐ | ☐ | ☐ | ☐ | ☐ |

During an argument: I want to resolve the issue right then and there.
☐ ☐ ☐ ☐ ☐ ☐ ☐

Sharing my marital issues with my biological family is important.
☐ ☐ ☐ ☐ ☐ ☐ ☐

Sharing my marital issues with my friends is important to me.
☐ ☐ ☐ ☐ ☐ ☐ ☐

Seeking marital counseling if needed.
☐ ☐ ☐ ☐ ☐ ☐ ☐

Saving money is important to me.
☐ ☐ ☐ ☐ ☐ ☐ ☐

Vacations are important to me.
☐ ☐ ☐ ☐ ☐ ☐ ☐

I love spending time with family/ friends.
☐ ☐ ☐ ☐ ☐ ☐ ☐

Decisions about me are my decisions.
☐ ☐ ☐ ☐ ☐ ☐ ☐

# A COVENANT

A covenant, when speaking of marriage, is when two individuals come together to form a life-long bond. One of the unique things that differs between a Covenant and a Contract is that a Covenant is forever binding, *to death do us part*. It's when the strengths and weaknesses of two individuals come together as one to become stronger in every area. Where one is weak, the other is strong. My wife is better equipped in areas that I struggle in, so as one united entity, I am strong because of her strength in that particular area. Her or my weaknesses are not a topic of fault-finding that she or I point out and criticize. If so, the one who criticizes is not fulfilling his or her obligation to the covenant agreement. They are failing to do their part by being the strength in that area. Each has been equipped by God with divine cures for each other's healing. We have been specially designed by God through life experiences to be the cure for each fault. Many unions dissolve, not because the two in the union are incompatible or no longer satisfy each other's needs or have character flaws. It is because they fail to understand their roles in the covenant agreement.

Now that you have individually completed this questionnaire, please arrange to meet with a professional counselor, your pastor, a mature married couple/person, or together as a couple, and discuss each item.

Created and Published by Charles Quinn, 2007, revised 2018.

# Note from the Publisher

## Are you a first time author?

Not sure how to proceed to get your book published?
Want to keep all your rights and all your royalties?
Want it to look as good as a Top 10 publisher?
Need help with editing, layout, cover design?
Want it out there selling in 90 days or less?

## Visit our website for some exciting new options!

www.chalfant-eckert-publishing.com

Made in the USA
Monee, IL
31 July 2023

40247488R00037